D1716828

Climate Scientist

by Elizabeth Noll

BELLWETHER MEDIA · MINNEAPOLIS, MN

Blastoff! Readers are carefully developed by literacy experts to build reading stamina and move students toward fluency by combining standards-based content with developmentally appropriate text.

Level 1 provides the most support through repetition of high-frequency words, light text, predictable sentence patterns, and strong visual support.

Level 2 offers early readers a bit more challenge through varied sentences, increased text load, and text-supportive special features.

Level 3 advances early-fluent readers toward fluency through increased text load, less reliance on photos, advancing concepts, longer sentences, and more complex special features.

★ **Blastoff! Universe**

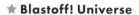

Reading Level

Grade
K

Grades
1–3

Grade
4

This edition first published in 2023 by Bellwether Media, Inc.

No part of this publication may be reproduced in whole or in part without written permission of the publisher. For information regarding permission, write to Bellwether Media, Inc., Attention: Permissions Department, 6012 Blue Circle Drive, Minnetonka, MN 55343.

Library of Congress Cataloging-in-Publication Data

LC record for Climate Scientist available at: https://lccn.loc.gov/2022005453

Text copyright © 2023 by Bellwether Media, Inc. BLASTOFF! READERS and associated logos are trademarks and/or registered trademarks of Bellwether Media, Inc.

Editor: Betsy Rathburn   Designer: Andrea Schneider

Printed in the United States of America, North Mankato, MN.

Table of Contents

A climate scientist is studying a river. She walks through the **currents**.

She notes the **temperature** of the water. She takes **samples**. Later, she will study them in a **lab**!

samples

4

What Is a Climate Scientist?

Climate scientists study Earth's weather over time. They collect and study **data** from around the world.

Their work teaches people about weather. It also teaches about **climate change**.

Famous Climate Scientist

Name  → James Hansen

Born → March 29, 1941

Birthplace
└→ Denison, Iowa

Schooling  → University of Iowa

Known For  → warned about the dangers of coal and oil to the climate

Climate scientists work at businesses. They work at schools. They work for the government.

They use math and science to do their work. They use computers, too. These help them study data.

Climate scientists take soil and water samples. They measure gases in the air. They look at how **glaciers** melt.

They note changes in weather. They look at changes in wildlife.

glacier

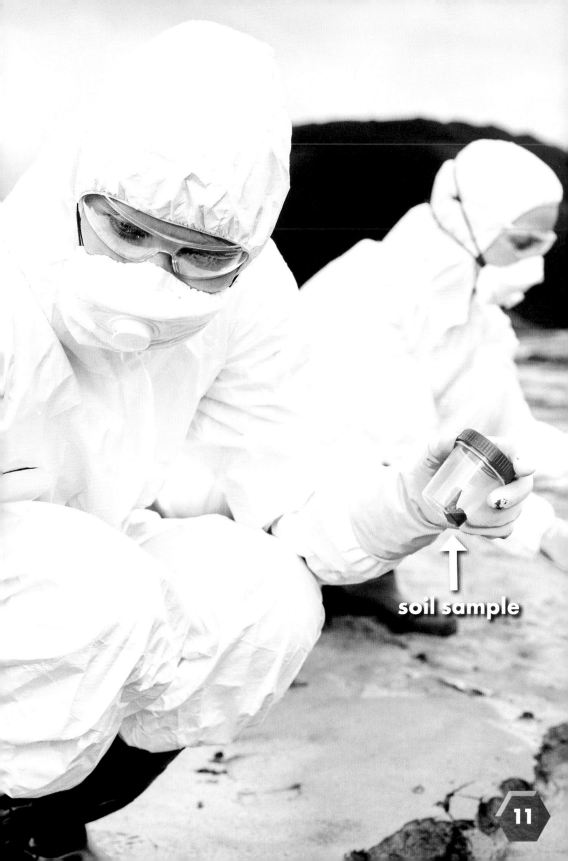

soil sample

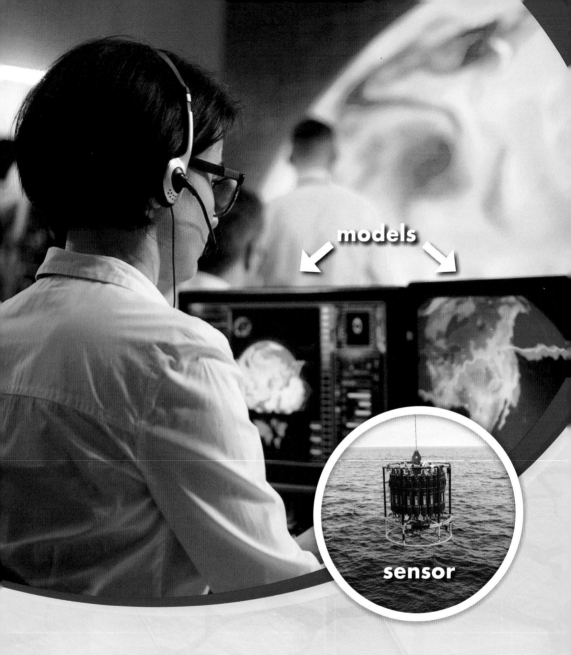

models

sensor

Many tools help them do their work.
Computers help make **models**.
These show Earth's future climate.

Sensors measure water levels. They tell how warm water is. Some climate scientists work to make better sensors!

Climate Science in Real Life

better crops

plans for natural disasters

long-term weather predictions

13

Their work helps them **predict** the future climate. They share how it will affect people and wildlife.

Using STEM

Science — test questions about climate change

Technology — use computers to make models

Engineering — design new sensors

Math — use past and present data to predict future data

CONFERENCE DE HERVE LE TREUT

LE CHANGEMENT CLIMATIQUE ET
LES ENJEUX DE LA COP 21

LYON LE 7 OCTOBRE 2015

climate scientist speaking
about climate change

They explain the dangers of
climate change. They tell how
people can slow the effects!

Becoming a Climate Scientist

Climate scientists should be good at **research**. They need good computer skills.

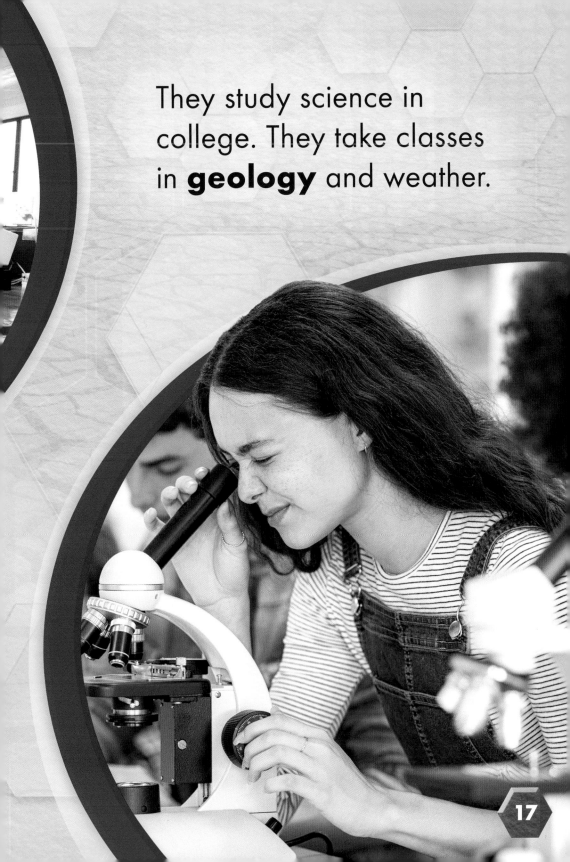

They study science in college. They take classes in **geology** and weather.

Some climate scientists go to **graduate school**. They choose a topic to research further. They write papers. They work in labs.

They work with **expert** scientists. They help with other scientists' research.

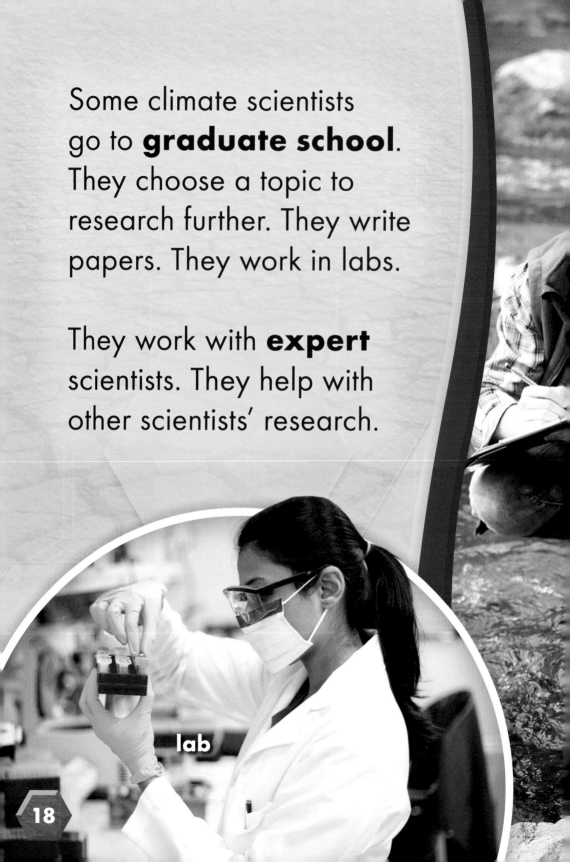

lab

In time, they are ready to lead their own research. They get jobs in labs. They work at schools. Some travel to collect samples.

How to Become a Climate Scientist

1
└● study science in college

2
└● research a topic further

3
└● work with expert climate scientists

4
└● get a job as a climate scientist

These scientists help us
understand Earth's future!

Glossary

climate change—a human-caused change in Earth's weather due to warming temperatures

currents—water or air moving in certain directions

data—information

expert—having a lot of experience in something

geology—the study of what Earth is made of

glaciers—massive sheets of ice that cover large areas of land

graduate school—a school where people can study a specialty area after college

lab—a building with special tools to do science experiments and tests

models—systems or processes that help scientists make predictions

predict—to make a guess based on data about what might happen in the future

research—careful study to find new knowledge or information about something

samples—small amounts of things that give information about where they were taken from

sensors—scientific instruments that can measure changes

temperature—a measure of heat and cold

To Learn More

AT THE LIBRARY

Barr, Catherine, and Steve Williams. *The Story of Climate Change: A First Book About How We Can Help Save Our Planet*. London, U.K.: Frances Lincoln Children's Books, 2021.

Minoglio, Andrea. *Our World Out of Balance: Understanding Climate Change and What We Can Do*. San Francisco, Calif.: Blue Dot Kids Press, 2021.

Neuenfeldt, Elizabeth. *Greta Thunberg: Climate Activist*. Minneapolis, Minn.: Bellwether Media, 2022.

ON THE WEB

FACTSURFER

Factsurfer.com gives you a safe, fun way to find more information.

1. Go to www.factsurfer.com.

2. Enter "climate scientist" into the search box and click 🔍.

3. Select your book cover to see a list of related content.

Index